Four Refrains

John Watson

Four Refrains

Acknowledgements

'Four Ways to Approach the Numinous'
won the Blake Prize for Poetry in 2009.

Four Refrains
ISBN 978 1 76109 127 8
Copyright © text John Watson 2021

First published 2011 by Picaro Press

This edition published 2021 by
GINNINDERRA PRESS
PO Box 3461 Port Adelaide 5015
www.ginninderrapress.com.au

Contents

Magritte Poems	9
Opening Salvo	10
The Same Salvo	10
Scene-Setting Haiku	10
Famous Joke	10
Recapitulative Haiku	11
Another Haiku	11
Couplet	11
A Surprise	11
Shunting Yards in the Hall	11
More Surprises	12
More Anachronisms	12
First Limerick	12
Recitative and Dénouement	13
A Samovar Too Far	13
Kicking Ahead	14
All That Glisters	14
Décor	15
Mysterious Limerick	15
Awkward Limerick	15
A Literary Reference	16
Limerick Offering a Possible Rationale	16
But Do Go On	16
What Really Happened Next	17
Or Perhaps This	17
A Retraction	18
Conversation Minutes After the Kick Into Touch	18
Resumed Normality Suggests Another Haiku	18
At Ease	19
The Kick in the Rear Viewed as Merely Figurative	19

Moving Right Along	19
In Conclusion	20

Four Ways to Approach the Numinous	21
By the Mystery of Presence	21
By Embracing Multiplicity	22
By a Devotion to Objects	24
By Approaching the River	26

To Wislawa Szymborska	29

Phaedrus	50
Alert	51
Police Radio Report	51
Les Flics Scramble	51
Meanwhile the Artist Sleeps	52
Bad Hair Day	53
Childhood's Failure to Prepare the Accused For These Unexpected Rays	53
Six Artists	54
These Foolish Things	54
Ruffling	54
On the Kisser	54
A Woman Under the Influence	55
Something in the Air	55
The Case for the Prosecution	55
Negative Capability	56
The Case for the Defence	57
Into the Radiance	57
Miss Rindy Sam Begs the Indulgence of the Court	58
Fluttering Induced by This Radiance; Further Defensive Notes	58
Variants on the Name 'Phaedrus'	58
Prose Poem 1	59

Prose Poem 2	59
The Search for Identity in the Presence of the Ineffable	59
Compulsive Tourist	60
Confession	60
Traveller	60
Prose Poem 3	60
Calibrations	61
A Previous Conviction?	62
In Her Own Right	62
Definitive Instance of Chopped up Text Lacking Expressive Force	63
Phaedrus Lounging in Sunlight	63
Mrs Mandarina Sam Breaks Her Silence	63
In the Heart of the Gallery	64
An Ancient Mariner to the Defence	64
A Peculiar Explanation	65
An Expert Witness	65
Rindy Sam Enthuses Without the Letter e	66
A Childhood Experience May Cast Light on a Later Compulsion	67
Soaring Lyric	68
Epilogue	68

Magritte Poems

for Richard Black

In the early days of his marriage he was alone in the house while his wife was in town with a friend.

The bell rings. It's the friend's husband, who has arranged to meet his wife at Magritte's house.

He introduces himself, as they haven't met before. He is highly respectable, bourgeois, an habitué of the casinos.

Magritte invites him in, steps back to let him pass and, the moment he sets foot in the drawing-room, gives him a tremendous kick in the backside. The astounded visitor hesitates between the multitude of reactions that come to mind, and in the end sits down as if nothing had happened on the chair which Magritte, as if nothing had happened, hastens to offer him.

– Soutenaire

Opening Salvo

A kick up the rear,
Slam dunk or grapple tackle;
Then with the utmost courtesy
A comfortable chair
And cucumber sandwiches.

The Same Salvo

Wrestled to the ground
Or kicked to kingdom come
By a maniac in a gorilla costume,
Then a soft cushion
And a reading from Thomas à Kempis.

Scene-Setting Haiku

Just inside the door
It is raining heavily;
Outside, the sun shines.

Famous Joke

Outside of a dog
A book is man's best friend.
Inside a dog it's too dark to read.

Recapitulative Haiku

A boot up the bum
Followed by the decorous
Offer of a chair.

Another Haiku

Introductions over,
The visitor gets the boot
Followed by high tea.

Couplet

The rough end of the pineapple,
Then a marzipan strudel.

A Surprise

The visitor collides in the drawing-room
With a train chugging out of the fireplace
But thinks nothing of it
Until he gets a boot in the broadbeam
And is startled, then is served
Petits fours and Darjeeling tea.

Shunting Yards in the Hall

The train has just juddered and shuddered
Into a nest of tables when
A sudden well-placed shot at goal
Finds the back of the net.

More Surprises

On his way down the hall
There are glimpses ahead of sunlight
Spilling over mountain ranges, glitter

Of Bakelite smoker's stand, traymobile
Drinks cabinet and tantalus…
Then he is struck forcibly

When out steps Johnny Depp
As if out of an avalanche.
Johnny Depp? Yep.

More Anachronisms

The visitor is elegantly attired
As if Axis-of-Elvis inspired;
He gladly suffers the kick up the bum
And seems not the least bit glum
Saying – You can do anything but please
Don't tread on my blue suede shoes.

First Limerick

Introductions completed, René
Asks the visitor in for the day.
        A quick kick to the rear
        And a chair is brought near
Then he's treated to *café-au-lait*.

Recitative and *Dénouement*

The visitor precedes Magritte.
He makes polite and boring conversation:
'Our two respective wives
Who are respectable and loyal
Are at the spectacle of the cinema.
For me the casino is the preferred receptacle
For my enthusiasms. Why, only yesterday,
I must tell you, at the tables
I had the remarkably good fortune to –
Ouch!'

A Samovar Too Far

From the hall during the moment before
The boot to the rear
The bourgeois visitor
Notes in the glittering sauna
Of the drawing-room's glare
A samovar too far.

Kicking Ahead

In 1913 at a fair
René met the fair
Georgette Berger.
In 1920 he met
Again, by chance, Georgette.
The mule-kick of fate
Propelled him on
Into the next room
To a midnight sun,
From now ahead of time.

All That Glisters

In the vestibule
A quick kick to the coccyx
And the offer of a comfortable chair
After which the visitor,

Somewhat uncertain as to the niceties of repartee,
Says only, 'Oh I see
You have a collection of framed Gary Glitter
Memorabilia. How the sun through the shutter

Catches the glitz.' 'No. In fact
These are glitterati, not to mention
Literati and arty practitioners.
But Gary Glitter is not amongst them.'

Décor

The visitor and René sit decorously
In the rearguard action's afterglow

While unknown to them in the city
In leaf-rustling Brussels of long ago

The two wives sit decorously
Nude for Paul Delvaux.

Mysterious Limerick

The guest cannot fail to observe
Odd anomalies touching a nerve.
      Fundamentally struck
      By a world come unstuck,
He sees pasts veering off in a curve.

Awkward Limerick

In the drawing room noting the clutter
And the sun bursting in at a shutter
      He is glad he has come
      Till a kick up the bum
Makes him unsure just what he should utter.

A Literary Reference

In the drawing room the guest
Going on ahead of his host
Was talking of the gods
Or rather their absence, and quoting
A sentence from *The Plumed Serpent*:

'This god stuff roars eternally
Like the sea, with too vast a sound
To be ever heard.' Meanwhile
He did not hear behind him
His host taking a flying punt.

Limerick Offering a Possible Rationale

What Magritte sought to see undergone
Was the *uncaused event*, or *frisson*,
      Or *complete disconnect*
    Which to have its effect
Must at no time be commented on.

But Do Go On

And so, I hear you ask, what happened next?
Just this: they sat, sharing a single thought
As if they watched a tree producing plums
And noted blossom, leaf, then budding fruit.

What Really Happened Next

Magritte spoke gravely to his guest
Now resting on a comfortable chair.
And scarcely remembering his pain.

'This is how we see the world,
Outside ourselves. And yet we have
Only an image of it here within.

Now are you seated comfortably?
For here comes the best part:
In just such a way we situate

From time to time in the past a thing
Which is actually happening now!
Is this not dazzling, marvellous and strange?'

Or Perhaps This

Magritte spoke to his guest:
'When I was twelve and unimpressed,
My mother who was still young

Drowned herself in the Sambre river
By leaping from the bridge. Her nightdress
Was completely covering her face.'

A Retraction

Although this circumstance
Might seem to explain
Certain veiled motifs in the iconology
In all its irrational variety,

It would be best to discard
Any suggestion that this explanation
Was ever made or was made
After the free kick in injury time.

Conversation Minutes After the Kick Into Touch

'It's all about *attending* to the present.
Yes, not letting it slip into the past.
Lawrence again: "The moment I saw
The brilliant, proud morning light over Santa Fe,
Something stood still in my soul
And I started to attend."'

Resumed Normality Suggests Another Haiku

After the attack
Came the long tacit silence
Of the mountain pass.

At Ease

Except for the slight but odd sensation
That he was wearing someone else's spectacles,
The visitor began to relax.
His wife's friend's husband's
Manner was cordial. Things seemed
Better than a poke in the eye
With a burnt stick.

The Kick in the Rear Viewed as Merely Figurative

In this version of events
While the wives are happily shopping
And being served tea by a flattering waiter,
The visitor, scarcely through the door
And comfortably shown to a chair,
Is subjected to a four-hour illustrated lecture
On The Origins of The Unconscious.

Moving Right Along

It is dusk by the time the wives arrive.
In an unexpected development it appears
That both wives are named Georgette,
Both are wearing dresses of crêpe Georgette
And in the lion's roar of the rose window
The two seem virtually and virtuously indistinguishable.

In Conclusion

The visitor receives a kick in the behind
Without responding. Next he is shown paintings –
The reverse mermaid, the train steaming
Out of the fireplace, the back-to-front
Reflection in the mirror, the flying bread loaves,
The cloud bird, the granite cloud,
The gigantic shaving brush and comb,
The tuba on fire, the pipe that isn't –
He enquires politely,
'Have you always been a realist painter?'

Four Ways to Approach the Numinous

By the Mystery of Presence

Gabrielle d'Estrées and one of her sisters, both naked
Are standing in what might be a bath. Lining its sides
Are milk coffee cloths, gathered and pleated by water.
Upstage in the gloom a fully clothed woman is sewing.

On each side a red satin curtain is tied back
Allowing the viewer a clear frontal view of the two sisters,
Who seem expressionless or, to be perhaps more precise,
Are giving nothing away because the pressure of decorum

Requires them to restrain, contain but nevertheless be aware
Of a considerable cargo of physical and metaphysical truths.
Above the woman sewing is the lower half of a painting
Of male legs suggesting a depleted Mars in disarray.

But the sisters' reticence and a mysterious and pervasive air,
As if they breathed pure nitrogen, makes instances of symbolism
Difficult to identify. One sister holds a pale nipple of the other
Between thumb and index finger in a circle, the hand highly

Stylised like a Balinese dancer's. The other holds a ring,
Her own hand forming a second, almost identical circle.
Their four forearms make a separate formal geometry,
As if this tableau of arms in itself represented something

Like an epigram the viewer should be able to read but cannot.
Their breasts, which lie in a single horizontal line,
Are small, conical and, as it were, undemonstrative,
Like four mounds in a raked Zen garden.

It is as if time had stopped several minutes earlier – perhaps
At the moment the one reached out her right hand
To the other's breast. It appears, although this may seem fanciful,
That she is adjusting the vertical hold in some 16th century

Equivalent of a screen bombarded from behind by electrons
So as to achieve an unstable, shuddering stillness
In which nothing else other than this gesture is happening
And the viewer watches some unchanging studio test-pattern.

Two pearl drop-earrings are visible, one obscured on each sister
By their centralising gaze. An unsatisfactory permanence
Seems to exclude the possibility of any future action
Such as stepping from the bath or drying or smiling.

By Embracing Multiplicity

Seven roads diverge in a wood
And at their point of departure
An acolyte meets a Master and asks him, 'Master!
How should I decide which path to take?
I know that at the end of one is a voluptuous tavern;
Another contains a cinema of dreams; a third
Offers cyberspace access to the past;
Another has a coin-in-the-slot peep show
Of selected future events which, it is said,
Is fully interactive; another leads to the sea
With hire boats and a favourable breeze waiting;
Another leads to a pavilion in which there are
Extensive and documented views of this very place of departure;

Another leads through a wilderness which is constantly changing
So that none can predict for a moment
The experience which might be gained there –'
The Master replies. 'I know you too well. You ask me this
Expecting me to answer in an enigma or reversal
Of all your expectations of an answer, or propose
Staying very still here at this point of indecision
So that all seven roads flow gently back to you,
Or give you a method of visiting all at once,
Even perhaps pointing you (in the Borgesian use
Of the term) to an Aleph where All is One
And where the angels put on a large dance-fest
In a ballroom on the head of a pin – and you're invited.

Perhaps you half expect me to announce steps
Leading underground which circumvent all seven paths,
Or conversely ease you into the gondola of a balloon
In which you might rise serenely into the air
To let the winds take you everywhere and anywhere –
But you have become too dependent on such contractions.
You have relied too long on everything approaching you
In labelled clusters or packets or quanta.
You have become accustomed to assuming the atoms
Of events may be combined into the molecules
Of experience, and this is not necessarily so.
You view everything as problem and seek a solution.
You expect that from every diverging path
There will be bridges to others, and this also
Is not necessarily so. I could continue, pointing out
Other radical simplifications you have unwittingly – Ah!'

The Master observes that his words are having
The desired effect: the acolyte's head is nodding
With weariness at so many words of reply; he leans
Against the broken and loosely turning signpost.
And soon the Master notes with satisfaction
(To a degree not incompatible with his humility as Master)
That the acolyte has fallen into a peaceful sleep.

By a Devotion to Objects

Morandi crossed the borders of Italy into the wide world
Twice only, and one of these occasions was to see
Paintings on the shores of a Swiss-Italian lake.
Otherwise he was frequently in his room allowing
His thoughts to gather dust and eliminate glare.

It is pleasing to imagine oneself actually standing
In that room (a bedroom) in front of a table
On which the votive objects stand. And to see oneself
Seeing them, like tourists in Rome for the Tiber spring flood,
Or viewing the Eiffel Tower with some degree of dispassion.

The objects are a group of bottles or canisters
Or ointment jars standing on a shelf
Crowding together like cows in a field, lowing,
Lowering their gaze, looking up, chewing cud,
Staring curiously behind a simple wire fence.

The still lifes made from this array are as familiar
As a coat hanging in a hall, and one need remark merely
On the propensity for that frieze of containers
To discourage, deny, descry any implication
That they contain anything at all, or that

They were assembled to assert in any way
Anything symbolic, allusive, shamanistic, allegorical,
Even nostalgic or tinged with sadness. Rather
It would appear they have arrived, jostled slightly
Then settled to attempt to profess essence merely.

Similarly one might consider one of several
Outdoor scenes. For instance here is something close
To a square representing the side of a house
Bordered by a dissemblance of trees like hair
And what looks like a trapezoid of ploughed ground,

That wall windowless, a churned-ricotta-white
With the tree backing off lest its shadow
Assume greater moment than its canopied branch.
Some claw marks partly distinguish the wall
From a rhombus of brown-purple (a field).

So reticent are these shaded areas with shadows
Posited in the gestures of eucalypt or conifer
One might well be in the afternoon lace cloth interior
Of the room in its Bolognese cool with the footfalls
Of three sisters elsewhere in the echoing house.

One would like to press further into this subtropical, leafy
Interior, this haven of shadows, and ask the reader
Stationed as he is at the apex of a triangle
Whose other vertices are these meditations and Morandi's tableau,
To allow these two to overlap and coalesce further,

As the eyes focusing after a reverie recombine
Two adjacencies into a single and singular éclat,
With the clarity of the gaze from a window
At the unflinching presence of umbrella pines like clouds
On an autumn afternoon in a rising breeze.

By Approaching the River

Towards the general wellspring of recollection itself
An instinctive resistance to being drawn surfaced, as if,
Once on display there, all original impulses must fail;

Or perhaps there was a desire to prevent the fall,
Into the general wellspring of recollection itself,
Of the floating world which so innocently, so vulnerably,

Was passing, intact and entire and magisterial:
The river surface, for instance, like a titanium mirror
Undisturbed, impossibly large, where siftings of rain already fell,

And a pelican single and solitary was indecisive about
Arrival and take-off with a little track of wake
Attesting to the intermittence of its resolve. O

How the general wellspring of recollection itself
Wants to take such epiphanies from the bystander
But does so peremptorily, is careless in taking

The choicest fruit from the centre of the pyramid,
So that the edifice pauses before collapsing suddenly
And spills out over the surrounding lawns,

Out of the general wellspring of recollection itself
And into the increasing disorder of Lost Property
Where float worlds of simulacra and dockets and motes.

But to the river! whose two divulged items, bird and rain,
Were tiny portions of an indivisible and larger whole:
These now threaten to overturn their floundering vessel,

For being singled out inevitably ties weights to the rest
And throws them overboard in a tangle of floating and sinking.
The boat rocks dangerously. And yet of course

There was no boat to be seen on the original river, nothing
So graspable or large. For some minutes before the first
Drops of rain the crows' Gesualdo madrigal veered

Somewhere amongst trees on the opposite bank;
The wrens' tiny flit and flight amongst aniseed trees,
A heron flying overhead just when items of similar degrees

Of granulation seemed to have been skimmed cleanly
From the surface of the eventful world; shimmers where
A fish may or may not have leapt, circles fading

Like the general wellspring of recollection itself,
And reflections – most ambiguously falling between
Incident and steady state – reflections of hinterland

Lowered in competing layers and of the blue torn openings
Between clouds, a stronger blue as reflections than above them.
And sounds! On the one hand the sound of grass

Being twisted then torn by a cow's tongue
Just behind the matted fence, and, on the other,
The sound like an improvisation for pins and pincushions

Of the rain falling lightly across the whole water sheet.
With the thought that exhaustive description may render appearances
Less susceptible to being made metaphor, the river divulges

Incident after incident: the stained grey tarpaulin looses
Tiny spiralling orbits, leaves moving in a slow convoy, aggregates
Of pollen; and the river announces a momentous event:

It is quasi-noon. The slow drift of tidal water
Hesitates, about to change direction, as if to reverse
The general wellspring of recollection itself.

To Wislawa Szymborska

1

Before I ask you for this dance
Perhaps I should confess
That I've had a previous infatuation
With Miss Moore.

2

And Marianne was
– I must be totally honest –
Great fun, especially in those harebrained
Afternoons at the zoo
Or skylarking amongst lotus trees
Or capering with goats.
(Capra (L) = goat.)

3

She did have an uncanny
Nonchalance with events
And could see similarities
Between the patina of water
And that of the wolverine's coat;
She seemed to have devised a method
Of siphoning and packaging them
To resemble peonies.

4

And it was actually she
Who, after cavorting with sailors
At Coney Island, finally
Found in me the telling absence
Of the mystique of the panda.

5

Therefore I must admit
To being in large part
Damaged goods – other planets' ash,
Electrons entirely recycled,
Perhaps even ancient pasts reconstituted.
This being fully declared
I press my suit.

6

You are looking away!
Have I lost your attention so soon?
Perhaps I should begin again
In the manner of Oscar Levant's
'I knew Doris Day before she was a virgin.'

7

For then, with a fresh overture
Knocked out as hectically as Rossini's
A few minutes before the curtain,
The old sinfonia might pass muster,
Might pull the wool
Over a few more eyes.

8

Prefaces to translations
Of your charming poems
Often include this claim:
'Few of the following
Have been previously translated…'
In fact several appear
To have freshly appeared in a snowfield
Or to have just been written
With the ink still glistening
Or written so faintly in window dew
That first light mistakes them
For a bowl of fruit.

9

But this sort of pussyfooting
And these sheepish attempts at compliments
May be way out of line;
Nevertheless I must press on regardless
Hoping to win your regard.

10

At our first meeting
I am unduly, immoderately, absurdly
Excited, nervously holding
And folding a felt hat,
And brushing back my hair,
But am startled out of these superficialities
To find your hand
'Miraculously feathered by a fountain pen.'

11

I must accept too
That, as one travels,
The log-book of days swells
As if it had fallen into water.

12

Impanate: to embody in bread (rare).
Despite (or perhaps because of) this rarity
This is what you do –
Sweetmeats rolled in breadcrumbs.
Devotedly I importune.

13

As our barouche crosses centuries
And trees resemble past dusks

You remark on the sea cucumber
And its capacity when threatened

To divide itself, surrendering one half
While elaborating on the second;

And I exclaim – Would that I
Could do this with a body of work!

14

Of course you have observed this:
That Lethe's trees cast shadows
Which are more luminous
Than the surrounding open fields.

15

Starlit one,
Would you honour me with presence –
Yours if such a possessive
May be binding in this avenue of locust trees (*Robinia*) –
And, if not, that of moonlight's shadow?

16

Walking down a flitter aisle of poplars
I'm endeavouring to explain how greatly I admire
Your nitpicking modes, your readiness
To stop in mid-metaphor and walk or fish
Or slice a cucumber or bounce a ball
Or chop parsley or pound
Rose petals with a pestle.

17

You raise your eyebrows and perhaps smile
(The loquat tree shadow
Is too dazzling for me to be sure)
And are possibly not listening. I repeat myself:

18

We're wandering in a green comb or coomb,
We've descended into a river valley.
Trees cast brilliant shadows.
You bend to the pebble-dry ground
And judiciously place a comma,
While I find a small rift
In the tumulus between two bluffs
Which is ideal for a semi-colon.

19

'Sacred folly of description!' (*Clochard*)
I would rather proceed without
The requisite detail, avoid too much
Of this foolishness, allow description
To trail behind us like a trawl net.
We walk down an avenue of laurels
And arrive at a strange building:
It is the Sacred Folly of Description.

20

You raise eyebrows of course by the utter
Simplicity of what you say:
And while I am too inclined to open
The hydrant of praise,
You note a tentative Hydra.
So, to catch your attention on the thornbush
Of the paths by the river – the past,
I quote the following long-distant lines:
'Everything they foresaw turned out quite differently
Or somewhat differently which also means quite differently.'
And I am encouraged by your declaration
'…that whatever I am to do
Will be changed into that which I have done.'

21

Passing a low range of hills
Such as those in whose shadow
We lived once in youth,
We note the complete absence of full stops.

22

In a dream I wandered
Quite irrationally
Over a forest of numbered leaves,
Spelling out as I walked
A provisional decimal for pi
– The same decimal you arrive at
In your poem on the same subject –
Until I could no longer find my way.

23

After another late night of television
(The *Lassie* movie and couch potato *Mash*
Were beguiling, since they signalled
The brimming bowl of time undiminished
By my ladle, my oars) I am
A little tired and late for our Readathon.

24

You have brought one of those poems which suggest
A Chopin mazurka arranged
By Pee Wee Hunt and His Orchestra
Or even Spike Jones in evening mood,
But I find that I have nothing
But the clothes I am standing up in.

25

Later our conversation takes off:
'On the way here' (I offer)
'I saw a man running for a train;
About to board, he saw the fountain pen
He had dropped on the platform
And, by retrieving it, missed the train.
On that train, I might add,
Everyone spoke a language
I could not understand nor even identify.'

26

'That's nothing,' you counter
With the tiger lily's bravura,
Not meaning to be dismissive
But rather to point up
The purity of all experience,
Its insularity from all but
A superficial osmosis,
A slight blurring of edges.
'On my way I saw an umbrella
Very like the one I reported,
In "A Speech in the Lost and Found Office",
Lost on the tramway. It was inverted,
Open, and floated down a flooded river;
Peering over its serious bulwarks
Was a small dog – a fox terrier –
Who wagged his tail upon seeing me.'

27

This part of the forest
Is particularly significant for me
For it is here on this very tree,
The silver birch of all trees fairest,
That Marianne carved her name.

28

Certain things belong absolutely to others –
The bleak grounds of the research laboratories
To Auden, to take an obvious instance;

And I must single out this herd
Of rare creatures hoof-shifting, shyly staring
– Animals infrequently mentioned in any taxonomy –

As Marianne's. And this pail of water
Shuddering violently as a result
Only of raindrops falling from a white sky

Must be the property of Tarkovsky. You are kind,
But I see clearly you have decided
That I have failed to annex any such territory.

29

On the way here by ferry
We docked; the white rope was very
Compliant in securing us. A young man
Boarded and pointed to someone who still ran
Towards the gangplank. It was a young woman
Who, strangely, wore the white orlon cardigan
So mandatory in the 60s and
Held it closed with one hand.
She boarded. She thanked the dockhand. We cast off.

30

– The enigma of the digital camera
And the incrementation of time!
– What? – This is the title of my thesis.
What do you think?

– Can you explain? – Certainly.
I mean, you have a digital camera,
I have a digital camera
As do an entire legion

Of Japanese teen-age girls.
As we approach the Opera House by water
We are all looking at our screens;
No one is looking at the Opera House itself.

– Can you expatiate further?
– I think so, yes. We have here
A veritable frogs' chorus of arrested glimpses,
A forest of baffles, barriers, checkpoints

Through which time's courier must run.
Many poems – most poems – assemble
These images of, say, Opera House and selected
Compatriots smiling in its gunwales;

In yours however several of the girls
Wear kimonos and appear to present
A Noh scene or two
For the delectation of ferry commuters.

31

I'm lying half asleep
And am half inclined to transfer
Half or more of my vague body of thought,

An unstable collection of ingredients,
Amongst them a whale sighting out to sea
And a seagull pecking at a shallows apple,

To you, with half a mind then to increase
The number of these fragments so that instances
Merge into generality; I would then hope

You would make of them one of your famous
Flourless cakes for which there is no recipe –
The cake with lemon zest and egg whites in peaks. Yes?

32

The sound of cicadas
Like a very long string of kelp beads;

A blue trampoline under leaves
Outside a blinded house…

Have I managed to make it sufficiently clear
That this takes place in summer?

Have I managed to make
A few particulars stand for something more?

Well, to be candid, no.
Could you begin again?

Very well. At the road sign pointing to *Lois Lane*
I determined to make a superhuman effort
To resolve all these questions.

33

In the Novelty Card Emporium
I search through hundreds of cards
All wrongly classified under *Humorous*.

Then I find this. On the front:
'Experts say not getting enough sex
Can make you hostile'

Then, inside, in strident printing
'Happy stinking
Birthday jerkface.'

34

So, is this – I ask –
So different from the familiar
And unfamiliar devices of poetry?

Well no, in the sense
That one is being asked
To make a deduction

Or draw a conclusion.
But yes, in that
No nymphs have departed.

35

In a notable poem
You knock at the door
Of a stone and, despite
Frequent attempts, get no reply.

Shall we together make
A fresh assault on the ramparts
Of the stone and demand
That it confess totally?

36

Now, shall we have a picnic *al fresco* with sherbets
And lemonade in glasses with little umbrellas
And glacé fruit, and ask your sister to honour her promise
As recorded in your poem 'In Praise of My Sister'
To relate her *much much much to tell*
On returning from her vacation in exotic places?

All of this would be, we realise, entirely dependent
On her not having written poems and on
Her having no intention of writing them, something
You have articulated with confidence repeatedly,
Assuring us that your sister has never written
And in all probability never shall write poems.

Let us then during this proposed picnic,
As we garnish with rocket and basil and baby
Spinach slices of salted tomato on water biscuits
And open small waterfalls of pink champagne
And set out portions of sponge cake with cream
And put on funny hats folded from serviettes.

Let us press her to relate her vacation secrets
And let us note these fugitive and fragmentary incidents
– The octopus rescued from a tidal pool,
The puzzling message pinned to the cabin door,
The impossibly permanent mulberry stains on beige shorts,
The tide so unusually far out something seemed wrong –
And regard them as if they were poems after all.

37

'The book of events
Lies half open'

With a few pages turned down.
– *I wish you wouldn't do that;*

It is bad enough
To note completed pages dog-eared

But perplexing indeed to find
Unread pages already turned down.

38

Let us agree to use the word
'Desuetude' more frequently.

Let us endeavour to use the words
'Diurnal' and 'quotidian'
On an almost daily basis.

Let us each write as many lines
Containing the word 'crepuscular'
As we can before it is too dark to write.

Outside the window in a mist
The trees move mysteriously
Like underwater branches:
Who will be the first to slap
On the table their matching image and call 'Snap!'?

39

When I was courting Miss Moore
I would delight in finding her name
Carved in bulwarks, sundials, nectarine wood.

Now sandstone whorls, swirls
Of Brownian skies
Or thumbprint cirrus skies
Or coral or undersea trees
Or even the simple resemblance
Between an initial glance
And a confirming one –

All of the above
I like to think bear
And bare your imprimatur.

40

People might say
'You have told us about one
Little thing happening and then
After only a slight refreshment
Another little thing happening, then
After a pause no larger
Than a man's cloud, another little thing
Uniquely happening. And we are
Wondering if you might be going
To provide some sort of development
Or – you know – connecting link?

For, if not, we are a bit inclined
To wander about or go
For a swim underwater and
Look at whales funnelling krill
Or seaweed sunning itself.'
But I beg to differ
And would like to distance myself
From such views. I, myself,
Speaking personally, am eager
To continue indefinitely reading
Any number of views with any number
Of grains of sand in the comfort
Of my eyrie in the planetarium
Of things which are simply themselves –
Things which lead you to the important –
Nay, highly important conclusion,
'When I see such things I am no longer sure
That what's important
Is more important than what's not.'
(No Title Required)

Coda

Finally we come into a little glade – or shade
– We may need a readiness to rhyme –
With heavy doors to be pushed open,
Lawn rollers, coal trucks on rails, strollers,

A wheelbarrow filled with coals,
Even a yacht with inert sails,
And you brandish (or, rather, you
Mention discreetly and I brandish)
$$\cos \varnothing.$$

We make it a point in these negotiations
To pay special attention to $\varnothing$
And having leaned into our lever
Or put our shoulders to the wheel for a while,

A little further on, everything being,
As you know, ever further on in space (see that?)
And in time (remember?), while sensing the weight
Of heroic fables, we encounter stables

A strong man is raking out.
His task seems enormous. But you have a discreet
Word in his ear; it is, I imagine, about
Increasing $\cos \varnothing$.

Then we've hardly gone a mile
Before we come to a stile
And see Sisyphus rolling a stone and making
Hard work of it. But, as soon as you explain
$$\cos \varnothing$$

His burden becomes noticeably lighter.
Now, you know about $\cos \varnothing$
And the average oarsman bending to his oar
Knows about $\cos \varnothing$

But does the reader? Here then
For you, O innocent lectors
Is a potted palm held version
Of the theory of vectors
                              and cos Ø:

A force is diminished by a factor
Of cos Ø, decreasing as Ø increases,
Where Ø is the angle between
The direction of application

And the desired direction of the force.
Ah! So that is how physics
Diminishes our efforts! And makes our best
Least, unless Ø is kept small.

How small? Well, pretty small (look at
This graph) unless you want to crack a nut
With the full resources of a sledgehammer
Or reduce eloquent exertion to a stammer.

Consider then how cos Ø
Thwarts our labours if given half
A chance and why, shaping on this wharf
To turn the oiled turnpike

And lower the barge through the lock,
We must consider direction, torque
And therefore the economy of our every attempt.
You, of course, Wislawa, extreme expert

In such economies, displaying effortless grace
And ease of movement from one line
To the next, lean
Into such metaphor with such finesse

As to keep Ø always close
To zero so that your cos Ø is thus
Scarcely diminutive. You are therefore
Serene, powerful, direct, precise;

And when plush comes to shovel
You may bypass the choreographer's injunction
Which won Edward Gorey's approval:
When in doubt, twirl.

Phaedrus

In July 2007, French police were summoned to a modern art gallery at the Hôtel de Caumont in Avignon to restrain a visitor caught defacing one of Cy Twombly's paintings. Overcome by what she would later claim was the emotional intensity of a completely white canvas (which forms one panel of Twombly's triptych *Phaedrus*), Rindy Sam – a Cambodian-born French artist –leaned forward and kissed Twombly's work, leaving a bright smudge of lipstick floating in the emptiness. 'The red stain,' Sam insisted, as she was taken into custody, 'is testimony to this moment, to the power of art.'

– Times Literary Supplement

Alert

Calling all cars: Hotel de Caumont,
Avignon; suspect wearing Chanel,
in art gallery kissing Cy Twombly's
chaste central canvas panel.

Police Radio Report

Cy Twombly's canvas is completely white
or at least it was until now;
now it has a bright lipstick glow.

The suspect is Rindy Sam, Cambodian-born
French artist who leaned forward
to bestow the reverential kiss.

Officers are warned the suspect
may be charming, passionate, volatile, wayward,
charismatic, unpredictable, vulnerable, agitated, aroused.

Les Flics Scramble

Several members of the French gendarmerie
were interrupted while itemising the armoury
when the call came.

Another was breaking petits fours into twos
and drinking coffee. 'There's no time to lose,'
shouted someone.

'Sacré bleu! Let's go,' (*en français*)
'A girl's kissing everything in sight, they say
in the Gallery.'

'She is? *Eh bien*! She sounds my type
and I hope this isn't just hype
for I'm a very visual person myself.'

Another: 'Let's arrest this *demoiselle* with heart.
I don't know much about Art
but I know what I like.'

Meanwhile the Artist Sleeps

Sombrely meanwhile, Twombly sleeps on in Rome
unaware that all his efforts
to protect the virginal white canvas
from the deposition of pigment

from particularities, from dispute,
from the application of meaning, from the inroads
of detail and the surrender to partiality –
his striving to allow nothing to stain

his immaculate and unconditional *Phaedrus* –
have come to nought at the lips
of an admirer. The work has become an advertisement
for passion, a used cocktail glass.

Bad Hair Day

The gallery owner has had a stressful night:
his partner has found lipstick on his shirt.
And he has felt all day
the ground unsteady at his feet.

It therefore comes as no surprise, to find this
strange willowy girl compounding his distress
by wobbling at that wall
and giving it a lipstick kiss.

Childhood's Failure to Prepare the Accused For These Unexpected Rays

In her childhood Rindy Sam
calmly stayed at home,
built towers from blocks
and heaped them with flowers,
played with crayons
and frayed rayons and silks,
was drawn to the moon…

But nothing, nothing

could ever prepare her
for the sheer
uncanny, irresistible, overwhelmingly
persuasive, unfathomable, impenetrable
canvas panel like moonlight,
a moon on which she just must
take a giant step.

Six Artists

Cy Twombly and Rindy Sam
are two well-known artists.
Wobbly Comb and Simply Randy
and Sky Sample and Cindy Ram
are four artists still awaiting discovery.

These Foolish Things

The day invites kissing,
the air offers its cheek;
remnants of dawn retain
lipstick traces et cetera, et cetera.

Inside the gallery
someone cries out:
the white noon sky
has acquired a sun.

Ruffling

People stand about afterwards and gawp.
Here's an unruffled lake
and surfacing, a bright orange carp.

On the Kisser

Although he's not normally grumbly
strange events can unsettle Cy Twombly
        when his *tabula rasa*
          gets a slap on the kisser
as a girl goes all suddenly trembly.

A Woman Under the Influence

In his triptych one panel was blank
thus holding back juice in the tank.
       But the girl was still moved
       to show she approved
with a kiss. Was it something she drank?

Something in the Air

A randy Cambodian, Rindy
who, it seems, was as bold as our Bindi*
       left a bright lipstick stain
       on Cy Twombly's clear plain –
Was it just that the weather was windy?

The Case for the Prosecution

I ask the court to contemplate
the effort Mr Twombly must have made
to check the impulse which in lesser hands

might well have led to trees and clouds
or figures in a landscape set with towers
or all those varied scenes which people paint

who can't resist to make their mark.
Had Mr Twombly wanted strawberry fields
or roseate petal bruising on his snow

---

* An enterprising Australian juvenile

he would have painted it. But no!
his self-restraint (where lesser men have failed
and filled the canvas with a thousand things)

this wanton smudge has not well served.
Your Honour, I submit this is an affront
to my client's high artistic reticence.

Negative Capability

As sunlight kissed the surface of the sea
and breezes touched up trees with sexual ease,
Miss Rindy Sam sought an epiphany,
some great configuration to amaze,

but nothing too prescriptive or precise.
In fact she felt a kind of hankering
for something unspecific, something nice
in being an open-ended kind of thing

where no one has decided this or that
or put his oar in. Where might this be found?
By chance the hotel gallery lay in wait
with just the item: Twombly in the round,
a triptych with one panel unspoiled. Yes!
The kind of pristine thing you *have* to kiss.

The Case for the Defence

Your Honour, I protest. My client's kiss
was quite Platonic – as it should have been –
since, as the court well knows, the work now smudged
is *Phaedrus*. And, I would submit,
my client did no more than humans do
who mark reflections on the firelit wall
from some white radiance, some pure Form
which in this case we may assume to be
the radiance Mr Twombly brought to bear
and whose bedazzling universal found
my client all too human in its blaze.
I rest my case, knowing the jury wise…

Into the Radiance

Clarion of whiteness,
negative of a photograph of a black hole,
dazzling beach into which I am drawn,
X-ray of the Exquisite Wrasse
imprinted in porcelain and held to the light!
To this Twombly assembly I humbly
submit without dissembling.
Humbly I press my lips,
bedewed with Chanel moisture
on to your lithe littoral or pectoral.

Miss Rindy Sam Begs the Indulgence of the Court

I thought for one mad moment
I was in bed with dear Hugo.
He is, you understand, so mysterious,
the silent type, so single-minded,
– how can I put it – so inexpressive,
I find him terribly exciting.

Fluttering Induced by This Radiance; Further Defensive Notes

Benign dragonfly helicopter over the hotel;
birdsong in the hoop pine hoopla;
intimations of cha-cha in the boudoir;
in the streets a barking Chihuahua.
No intensity of collapsar pulsar
no avatar, no amount of brouhaha –
even the beach at low tide in the absence of noon,
thistle blowing in the motionless air –

Nothing could prepare me for this revelation.

Variants on the Name 'Phaedrus'

Can Phaedra have any place here?
Are not her passions to be acknowledged
as she bends to kiss the sleeping torso of Hippolyte?
Is not this some amelioration
of the passion of Rindy Sam?

Prose Poem 1

This rockform is surely the one I climbed in childhood except that it cannot be, this being a portion of the coast some hundreds of miles further north. This expanse of beach is surely the very one I traversed, with the pools in which every fish was hiding always behind weed pinnacles and turrets and conical towers and yet it was in another country. I am confused by the splendour of these absences.

Prose Poem 2

At very low tide quietly the pink flesh of the rocks is revealed in the swaying motion of the beaded weed skirts. And here, in the gallery of the Hotel de Caumont, by an almost infinitesimal sideways shift, the same sway and swell of weed skirts reveals this redolent and seductive surface to which with all my heart I bend forward and give myself.

The Search for Identity in the Presence of the Ineffable

I'm known as Rindy Sam.
I'm Popeye the Sailor I yam I yam.
I've long been on the lam,
in search of the mystic yam,
the pearl in the giant clam;
I'm a fluttering oriflamme,
I'm a person without identity – I am,
lost in this hologram.

Compulsive Tourist

At this desert at dawn without paths,
I let my lips do the walking.

Confession

– I always thought I'd like,
confided Rindy Sam to her Fraternity,
to stain the white radiance of Eternity.

Traveller

I've travelled everywhere beneath the sun
and never thought to find
in Avignon the Blarney Stone.

A spotted dog was sleeping near the door,
a child played a celeste,
the gallery looked just as before.

Then there it was – a stubble field in the sun,
a lake in fuming light.
Held upside-down I kissed the Stone.

Prose Poem 3

Might one's curiosity upon first entering the hotel gallery leaving behind guests on the balcony and terrace drinking glasses of what looks like a seaweed coloured wine, might one's startlement at seeing the blank panel in the Twombly triptych be compared to the feeling of standing in what would once have been a few feet of water in the long-since abandoned and sea-broken rockpool? Blocks of masonry have been thrown against the cliff and lie scattered half buried in sand – blocks suggestive of the blocks detected at Rhodes which may well be fragments of the lost Colossus. Next to record is the similarity between this empty space formerly tidal pool with its wall now scattered about its floor, and the feeling of mounting entrancement at this empty panel resulting finally in the impulse to kiss the vacancies and leave lipstick traces on its startled cheeks.

Calibrations

Assigning a grid to the white canvas
so that it encompasses points
from A1 to Z30, it happens

Rindy Sam notices as she sways
Forward making lip contact a single hair
Attached at approximately the point M22.

She half forms the thought, almost
gratifyingly, 'Aha – so here we have,
after all, human accident!'

But this instance of a blemish –
if blemish it could be thought – in this field
cannot prevent her implanting the kiss.

A Previous Conviction?

The prosecution will further allege
the accused has faced a similar charge
on several occasions previously
deserving of the court's censure and philippic
for her looseness with lipstick.

In Paris when a stretch limmo paused
at traffic lights the accused
by a now familiar instance of wantonness
caused its dignitaries no little pain
by leaving on its door a crimson stain.

And once, it is said, in Belarus
the accused kissed a horse
on the flanks, in a field,
leaving a blaze of a strange shade.
No charges were laid.

In Her Own Right

In the early days of Cinemascope
O tempora, O mores!
we sat transfixed by the ceremonial
opening of the cinema curtains
to reveal a screen as long as a cloudless day
out at sea in an open boat.
Something of the same experience
of amazement must have seized
the volatile and ready-to-be-deliquescent
performance artist Rindy Sam.

Definitive Instance of Chopped up Text Lacking Expressive Force

Twombly's father also nicknamed Cy
after the baseball great Cy Young
pitched for the Chicago White Sox.

Phaedrus Lounging in Sunlight

The opening of Plato's *Phaedrus* in the Jowett translation
arbitrarily divided into lines: Socrates begins by asking
'Whence come you and whither are you going?'
Phaedrus: 'I come from Lysias the son of Cephalus
and I am going to take a walk outside the wall
for I have been sitting with him the whole morning
and our common friend Acumenus tells me
that it is much more refreshing to walk
in the open air than to be shut up in a cloister.'

Mrs Mandarina Sam Breaks Her Silence

The day was a blaze like a horse's mane
or a sail far away on a sea lane.
I am from Siam, yes I am,
where skies are of beaten gold,
and my niece would often, yes often, say
when she was still just a child
'Aunty! I want to embrace every day;

every day is like my face
in a mirror.' Well, this day
– as I say – was a pure blaze
and as my niece and I entered the hotel
intending to take cakes and tea, my niece
was already in a daze. We saw the gallery
and its panels and storm-tossed bays
like dusk over water. She freshened
her lippy in the powder room,
thinking perhaps of Lippi. I think
she was already back with those skies…

In the Heart of the Gallery

My back turned to the sea
and around my head the roar of bees,
I looked at a beach which was entirely empty.

Stars were racing (*Pasternak*)

I looked down wormholes into empty space
at glistening galaxies like melting ice.
I felt myself falling.

An Ancient Mariner to the Defence

'Blinded by the sun, she were –
I know that feeling well.
I've sometimes fallen to the deck
the albatross about my neck,
and looked at nothingness.

Poor girl she stared into the sun
too long, too long –
the genius blaze burns everyone.

And what is whiteness, Sir, if not
the jettison overboard
of every colour. There she stood
on deck, Sir, in a kind of daze
and looked at nothingness.'

A Peculiar Explanation

I felt strangely overwhelmed – as if, as if
I were a Bach Passacaglia and Fugue
and were being orchestrated by Leopold Stokowski.

An Expert Witness

As a critic I am frequently asked,
'What does it all mean?' and in reply
I would say that in this case
Twombly's grumbly and bumbly and crumbly line,
his jittering and flittering and skittering confusion –
or glittering and fluttering conflation –
of drawing and painting places a high value
– I'm not going too fast for you am I? No? –
on randomness and the accidental. Thankyou. And,
in the context of that particular ethos
the lipstick stain which comprises Exhibit A
may well be considered, accordingly, as mere static.

But having said this, with a nod or I might say
spatter in the great Greenberg's direction
I should stress that there are here
– ineluctably and indubitably – social concerns.
And thus I would direct your attention
to the well-known Connie Francis number 'Lipstick
On Your Collar' which I would contend so adequately
embodies the zeitgeist in this case.
I would place Cy Twombly's depiction of innocence
before or perhaps even – bravely – after the Fall
in his white panel or we might say latterly
panel van – as the wronged party;
and the defendant Rindy Sam as Grandslam Philanderer.
I see I am being signalled to pause,
But after the adjournment I hope to address
the ramifications of the theme *Lipstick as Weapon*.

Rindy Sam Enthuses Without the Letter e

I was foolish. I can say that.
But what can I say about this man
who has shown such daring
in confronting Nothing, inviting us
to party visually with him
without artificial stimulus? Oh, how natural
that littoral, how calm that plain!
I am sorry, your Honour:

I did not think my kiss
could result in such fuss
or hubbub. For on that day
I was only acting out my admiration
and acclaim for this bravura display
of radical holding back from all
obvious, banal or simplistic scratching.
But notwithstanding my guilt
(if guilt is found) I cannot but think
that although I lost control – I was so rapt –
in a passing sunspot or two –
in all I did I can find nothing
a bit of bicarb of soda wouldn't fix.

A Childhood Experience May Cast Light on a Later Compulsion

When I was five
and the chestnut tree was so alive
outside at the window

I leaned into the mirror
almost with a kind of terror
and with my mother's lipstick

saved myself from falling
into those appalling chasms
by kissing the cavernous glass.

Soaring Lyric

Ah, Cy Twombly's etiolated plain!
like Wembley Stadium on Cup Final Day
viewed by helicopter the helicopter soaring
until every detail of the crowd dissolves
and resembles the earth at the end of *Solaris*.

Epilogue

Let us all run out into the street
and adorn every surface with kisses.

Let us impulsively improvise dapple,
and delight in adding to the already

glacier scathed, windswept, cloud blurred, willow
shaded, rock-pool shimmering, cropped field world.

Let us map such Twombly moments,
and let us seek always to be trembly.

www.ingramcontent.com/pod-product-compliance
Lightning Source LLC
Chambersburg PA
CBHW062155100526
44589CB00014B/1850